When You Are Afraid

Saint Ansgar Ev. Lutheran Church
515 WOODFORD ST. at COLUMBIA RD.
PORTLAND, MAINE 04103

When You Are Afraid

A Book of Comfort

Alvin N. Rogness

Augsburg
MINNEAPOLIS

WHEN YOU ARE AFRAID
A Book of Comfort
by Alvin N. Rogness

1999 Augsburg Books Edition.

Text of this edition originally appeared in *Book of Comfort,* Copyright © 1979 Augsburg
Publishing House.

Cover design by Craig Claeys; interior design by Michelle L. Norstad.

Acknowledgments
Scripture quotations are from the New Revised Standard Version © 1989 by the
Division of Christian Education of the National Council of the Churches of Christ in
the United States of America. Used by permission.

Library of Congress Cataloging-in-Publication Data

Rogness, Alvin N., 1906-
    When you are afraid : a book of comfort / by Alvin N. Rogness. —
Augsburg Books ed.
    p. cm.
    Includes bibliographical references.
    ISBN 0-8066-3842-7 (alk. paper)
    1. Fear—Religious aspects—Christianity. 2. Christian life—
Lutheran authors. 3. Consolation. I. Title.
BV4908.5.R58 1999
248.8'6—dc21   98-48283
                                           CIP

The paper used in this publication meets the minimum requirements of American
National Standard for Information Sciences—Permanence of Paper for Printed Library
Materials, ANSI Z329.48-1984.

Manufactured in the U.S.A.   AF 9-3842

03   02   01   00   99   1   2   3   4   5   6   7   8   9   10

Contents

Preface

You and I are on a road of sharp turns and sudden dips. And there's fog, thick fog. Sometimes boulders block the way. We neglect the map and are lured into detours. Weary, we may want to give up. We cry for comfort.

There is comfort. Years ago God said,

> Comfort, comfort my people. . . .
> Speak tenderly to Jerusalem, and proclaim to her
> that her hard service has been completed,
> that her sin has been paid for,
> that she has received from the Lord's hand
> double for all her sins.

God yearns to comfort us—but on God's terms and in God's way. If I call on God, I understand that he may have to stop me in my tracks and turn me around before he can be gentle. God may have to use the scalpel before he can heal my pain.

In these short chapters I've tried to describe stretches along the road. I've traveled many of them. I'm old enough to have learned a little about them. But I'm no heroic traveler. Many times I've rejected God's comfort and tried to go it alone. Often I've been puzzled about the kind of comfort God seemed to give.

I have the map, the Word of God, God's wisdom and promises. And I have a Friend who has walked the way before me and who walks with me now. His hand is on me to lead me and to hold me. There is no greater comfort than that.

1

When Fear Paralyzes

Any kind of fear tends to immobilize. In its extreme form, terror, it paralyzes. You can't utter a sound, you can't move. Most fears are rooted in some circumstance, real or imagined, over which we have no control. A dog leaps out of the bushes to bite, a car veers into our lane, a forest fire sweeps toward us, we are awakened by stealthy footfalls in the dark. The danger is real. We fear.

There are also fears generated by something not dangerous at all. Small spaces, such as an elevator, make some people tremble. Others fear large spaces, such as prairies. In Rolvaag's Giants in the Earth, Berit, the immigrant wife, comes from Norway's mountains to the endless prairies of the Dakotas. She creeps into a large trunk and tells her husband, "out here there's nothing to hide behind and nothing to lean against."

Others are plagued by a pervading fear, like an overhanging cloud. They don't know why, or where it comes from. They want to escape, but they don't know from what. The fear may be rooted in some forgotten experience in the far past, and expert help will be needed to ferret it out.

My own encounter with fear that makes no sense took the extreme form of what is called "stage fright." As a junior in high school, one day I was reading a part of a Shakespeare play when the thought flashed through my mind, "Suppose I can't finish reading this paragraph." Suddenly I was in panic. I struggled to read on, but ground to a breathless halt.

My panic was senseless. I have good lungs, a good voice, and people are friendly. But from that moment on, through a lifetime, again and again I have fought that fear. In classrooms, as my turn to read approached, I sometimes found some pretext to leave the room. I considered quitting school. When I enrolled in college, I majored in chemistry and mathematics, determined to go into some work where I would not be called on to read or speak in public.

At one point I thought that God might be telling me something. When Paul prayed to be rid of his "thorn in the flesh," God chose to let him keep it, saying, "My grace is enough." Was God giving me one point of stark need, to remind me that in everything I must rely on him?

Though I ended up in an occupation in which I've been reading and speaking to the public most of my life, the fear has never left me. It lurks under the surface every time I face an audience, or even when I read the Scriptures to my family. Its paralyzing power is still there.

I suppose most of us know best the fears of the unknown—of a threatening future, for instance. The fear may be highly personal, such as fear of losing by death or betrayal someone we love. Or it may be more global, such as fearing a future where nuclear war, world hunger, the exhaustion of energy, and overpopulation loom like dark clouds on the horizon.

Ours is an age of that kind of fear. Never before has the world been so interdependent, never before have nations had such power to destroy, and never before have the media thrust these fears into the living rooms of every home. My grandfather, pioneering the prairies a hundred years ago, would read of crises in Moscow, London, or Washington two weeks after the event, and then probably on page three of his Norwegian weekly, without benefit of pictures, and with no effect on his blood pressure. He had blizzards and grasshoppers and drought to worry him, but not the collapse of the world.

Fear breeds hopelessness, and hopelessness paralysis. We are all tempted today to give up on the future, to eat, drink, and make merry in some grim way until the holocaust comes. We drive ourselves with short-range goals, such as making money or gaining power or pursuing pleasure. We wonder if long-range goals—righteousness and justice and purity of heart—have any value. And in the wake of giving up on abiding values, we give up on the dignity of the human being. Short-range passions take over, and unbridled pursuit of power sends six million to Nazi gas chambers. Unchecked clamor for wealth widens the gap between the haves and the have-nots, and unleashed pursuit of pleasure lures our youth into dangerous lifestyles.

How can God comfort us in this hour? God wants to. His heart must be breaking when he sees his children throwing their inheritance to the winds.

When I look for comfort, I try to remember some basic insights from Scripture. First, God is both merciful and just. If a child has broken the law and lands in prison, a good parent will not break into prison and help the child escape. The child must pay the just penalty. A good God cannot lightly dismiss our sins. Such indulgence would only speed us on to continued destruction. But God is merciful, and of infinite patience. God will not abandon us.

I remember a question from the edition of Luther's Small Catechism I used as a child: "How does God deal with us in our sins?" The answer given was, "He allows us to sin, but sets limits to our sinfulness."

I think that God is still in control, and that he has ways to turn us in our wretchedness—and history itself—around to a new direction. Evil plants the seed of its own destruction. It's not only the forces of righteousness that destroy evil; evil is self-destructive. The wheels of God grind slowly, but they grind surely.

Then, I dare not minimize the power of one person who is dedicated to God and to service in the world. Goodness is stronger than evil. History has many instances of this truth. Sir William Wilberforce at age twenty-one was elected to the British Parliament. Three years later he had a decisive encounter with God, and he considered leaving Parliament for "religious work." His friend, Pitt the Younger, persuaded him to stay and struggle politically against the legalized slave trade of the empire. Three

13

decades later, largely through the untiring efforts of Wilberforce, Parliament outlawed slavery and reimbursed slave holders twenty million pounds sterling out of the national treasury.

Who knows where in this very hour God is moving and equipping some individual for work that can reverse the flow of history! All of us have orbits in which we are invited by God to give ourselves to unselfish service for others, in our homes, in our churches, in our communities. Our little battles for justice and mercy may not be as dramatic as that of Wilberforce, but our Lord weaves them into the warp and woof of the whole. We become part of his leaven, that which keeps things from disintegrating and gives hope for the future.

When well-meaning people give up in pious despair and do nothing but sit around waiting for the Lord's return, the Lord must be displeased. We dare not let fear rob us of hope. The earth is the Lord's. This is part of his kingdom. It's not the final fulfillment, of course. God will give us a new heaven and a new earth. When, no one knows. Meanwhile, he has put us here to care for this one, and for one another.

"Let us, then, be up and doing, with a heart for any

14

fate," said Longfellow. There may be catastrophes, there may not. Asked what he would do if the world were to end tomorrow, Luther is supposed to have said, "I would plant an apple tree today." Ignatius Loyola, sixteenth-century founder of the Jesuit Order, as a student was playing a lawn game with two of his friends. One of them posed the question, "What would you do if the world were to come to the end in two hours?" One said, "I'd go to the temple and pray." The other, "I would go and be reconciled to my brother." Ignatius had been silent. They asked, "What would you do?" He replied, "I would finish the game."

God has put us here in this hour. We have work to do. Putting aside our fears for the long tomorrows, we live in a today throbbing with all sorts of opportunities for service in our little worlds. Remember the worlds of Hebrews 12: "Lift your drooping hands and strengthen your weak knees . . . . let us throw off everything that hinders us . . . . and run the race marked out for us."

> *"Do not let your hearts be troubled and do not be afraid."*
> *John 14:27*

2

When the Choice Is Unclear

A friend applies for a job and asks you to provide recommendations. You know he is a recovered alcoholic, but fear that if you include that information, he won't get the job. Should you, or should you not?

A house is on fire. The husband can save himself, but he cannot possibly save his invalid wife. Should he let her die, or should he stay and die with her?

A twelve-year-old boy was brought into the hospital, his leg riddled with shotgun pellets. Gangrene set in (before the days of penicillin). I watched a tortured father as the doctor faced him with the decision: Should he let the doctor remove the leg?

Several years ago a prominent American churchman and his wife died from an overdose of pills which they had taken in a mutual pact to end their lives when they were no longer able to contribute to the world. Each had become debilitated by an incurable disease that threatened to rob them of intelligence and speech. The whole Christian world puzzled over their choice.

At a conference on Christianity and economic decisions, Arthur Fleming, then chief of the Office of Defense Mobilization under President Eisenhower, asked how the church could help him in the hard decisions he had to make between Sundays. He said it was easy to decide that the Lord wanted him in church on Sunday to worship and to teach a class, to tithe, to have family prayers. But in the complex issues that faced him in his office, he was without clear direction. Who could help him?

Many people make choices with little or no thought for the will of God or even for moral principles. But those who want to do the right when the way is not clear may cry for some cable from heaven.

Are there any guidelines for tough decisions? I think so. Take a good look at the Ten Commandments. They are valid still, after all these centuries. And consult some person of integrity in whom you have confidence. From what you know about the life of Jesus, ask yourself what he would likely do in your situation. You have reason and common sense—use them. Remember, too, that Jesus was hard on the law-and-order boys of his day. Listen to your heart.

To fulfill God's laws, on one hand, and to show mercy to people, on the other hand, can bring us into difficult conflicts. In our complex society, we face baffling choices. We are left without absolutes, except in broad, sweeping principles. Even the familiar "Do unto others as you would they should do unto you" won't always hold. An alcoholic may give a fifth of whiskey to a fellow alcoholic because that's what he'd like to have done for him. That would be a gesture of goodwill, but hardly pleasing to God.

When you have marshaled all the wisdom you can and siphoned off as much self-interest as possible and you make the choice with every good intention, you may still have to be tentative enough to add a little prayer: "Forgive me, Lord, if I have misjudged what you wanted me to do." And God forgives!

If any of you lacks wisdom, he should ask God, who gives generously to all without finding fault, and it will be given to him.

James 1:5

3

When You Think
You're Not Needed

One of our deepest needs, perhaps the very deepest, is to be needed. This fact is a clue to something essentially fine about us.

To reach a point in life when no one needs us any longer is a frightening prospect. This is a fear for both old and young. Young people wonder if the world will have a place for them. Older people, about to retire, dread the thought that their time of meeting needs will soon be over.

If you gave young people a million dollars each and told them that they must loaf the rest of their lives, you would drive them to melancholy. Show wealthy older people brochures for endless travel, and they lapse into sadness. A friend of mine, recently retired and jetting from one resort to another, said, "Al, these swimming pools get old awfully fast."

I remember well when my sister, the youngest of our family of six, was graduated from college. I told my mother that it must be a wonderful day for her and dad. At long last they were through struggling with college bills. She replied, "We've often talked about that day coming and how nice it would be, but now that it's here, we're a bit sad to think that you don't need us any longer." At the end of another generation it is now my turn for sadness. Our six, too, have finished college.

There are other ways to be needed than paying college bills, of course, or, for that matter, working at a job. My parents lived twenty-one years beyond my college graduation, and they may not have known it, but in many ways they met my needs as fully then as before. When they died, both the same summer, they left a great ache in my heart and a yawning hole against the skyline of my life.

One of the deceits of our industrial civilization is to measure people's worth in terms of production. If they aren't producing food or shelter, health care or education, or the myriad of things people consume, they have a hard time rescuing any sense of importance. They become horses put out to pasture, obsolete machines, wards of the state, parasites on society. A consumerist culture puts them on a shelf to wait the day of the mortician.

Nor will they be rescued by another deceit, such as substituting hobbies and travel for work. That is nothing more than trying to make the shelf more tolerable. They need something else. They need to be needed.

As you grow older, you are needed—maybe not in the factory or office or wheat fields or operating room or school room, as you were before, but you are needed by every person who is lonely and discouraged, every person who is forgotten, every person who cries out for someone who cares. And there are millions of such, many in every community, whether they be rich or poor.

He never knew it, but I needed him. He was totally paralyzed with arthritis, lying in his bed like a board. Except for his alert, sparking eyes and his warm smile, he didn't move, but he had an inner radiance. I never left him but any lingering self-pity was smashed to bits. He put me on my feet again to face life with cheer. He was no obsolete machine. He may never have known how important he was to me and to others, but God knew. It must have been such awareness that led John Milton, blind at forty-four, to say in his ode, On His Blindness: "They also serve who only stand and wait."

For want of imagination, a person may fail to find the doors to others' needs. A pastor told me of a business executive who, upon retirement, was so bored that he kept drinking more and more. His wife soon joined him, and both were well on the way to becoming alcoholics. One day the pastor virtually compelled him to deliver some Meals on Wheels to elderly and sick people in the community. This did it! He became absorbed in the lives of these people who had escaped him during his busy executive days. Meeting the simple need of providing a car for the delivery of meals, he found doors opening for giving himself in ways he had never known. He needed neither hobbies nor travel nor martinis to brighten up his retirement shelf. He was off the shelf.

Jesus gave us the key long ago. "It is more blessed to give than to receive." What sheer fun it is to be able to fill another's need.

In a profound sense, we are of importance not because we are productive, not because we are needed, not because of anything we do or don't do. Our importance is given us as a gift from God. We are God's children, loved simply because we exist. We have worth because we are. We are justified by grace, grace alone, not by any inventory of works.

22

But God needs us. The Creator commissions us for a life of service. And his enterprises on earth have myriad openings, for old and young. To let ourselves be needed is to discover the riches of life with God.

> *Therefore, as we have opportunity, let us do good to all people, especially to those who belong to the family of believers.*
> *Galatians 6:10*

4

When You Fear Catastrophe

An eminent psychiatrist friend of mine once said that everyone lives with a sense of imminent catastrophe. Any moment one's world could fall apart.

In recent years I've sometimes awakened in the morning wondering whether the world would hold together another day. The problems are so great and the world so interrelated that if one part collapses, won't the whole structure crumble, like a house of cards, into total chaos? In this mood I dress, go to the kitchen for a cup of strong coffee, and read prayers that others have written (I couldn't put together a cheerful one for myself). By the time I get out with other people I have a feeling that the world will hold together, at least for another day.

Don't we all live with a feeling of catastrophe around

the corner? My friend is right. A heart attack could fell me. I could get a telephone call that one of my children or grandchildren has been killed.

We were totally unprepared that night of August 18, 1960, when two policemen came to our door to tell us our son Paul was killed. In the years following, whenever our children and grandchildren are due to arrive, I'm a bit uneasy until they're at the door, and when they leave I'm nervous when the telephone rings until I know they're safely home.

It's not that I'm semi-paralyzed, thinking of the worst that could happen, but tucked down somewhere in my consciousness is the awareness of the uncertainties of life.

Nor was it Paul's death alone that brought this awareness of the catastrophic. I was seventeen when five of the seven banks in Sioux Falls closed their doors in 1923. That same year my father's store burned to the ground one dry, October night. In 1929 the stock market crash sent the country and the world into unprecedented hard times. And during the war in the 1940s I shared the fears of families in my congregation who lived daily with the dread of a telegram: "It is with deep regret that the office of the U.S. Army informs you that your son. . . ."

25

The world has always lived with the sense of possible calamity. But it seems to me that in recent decades, in spite of unrivaled economic affluence in our land, the fear of both domestic and worldwide collapse has been fueled in new ways. I'm not at all sure why this should be so.

The nuclear bomb is new, of course. Thousands of Hiroshimas could mean the end of civilization. Recent calculations of how soon the earth will run out of life-sustaining energy, water, air, and food also create a sense of looming disaster. Then there are the religious "readings of the times" that carelessly use Scripture to spell doom.

It is an offense to God to give up hope and to live as if our history is but one catastrophe after another building up to one final, colossal holocaust. Anticipation of Christ's return and a "new Jerusalem" comes not from weariness with struggling against the evil forces in this world. It comes from the promise that this world at its very best is but a glimpse of something infinitely more fulfilling to come. Longings for God's heaven come not from a repudiation of God's earth, but from hunger for the goodness and beauty that we have tasted here.

It is unworthy of us as Christians to be apostles of doom, always looking into the tomorrows of impending misfortune. Misfortunes will come, but they need not spell collapse. Most of our fears do not materialize. When they do, we are not abandoned. God is with us, and as he told the apostle Paul, "My grace is sufficient." With him we will weather the storms. Even if the world blows up, it is not the end. We are eternal beings. God, who raised up Jesus, will raise us up (if we will let him) and give us life anew in the more glorious sector of his kingdom.

We are not wise enough to know that the world is on a roller coaster to disaster. There may be golden days ahead, before Christ returns. The age-old enemies—disease, hunger, and war—may lose some of their power.

Will Durant, renowned historian-philosopher of our century, on his ninety-second birthday deplored the decline of religious belief and of the disciplines of our earlier rural society. He struck a final note of courage, however:

> I will not end on this plaintive note. I still believe in
> you (in people) and in America and in Europe. . . . I
> believe that there is a creative spirit in the universe—
> in every atom, in every plant and animal, in every
> man and woman—a spirit evident in history, despite
> every setback and disaster. I believe that the human

27

heritage, in technology, government, education, literature, science, and art, is greater than ever before, is better protected, and widely spread, than ever.

Whenever the dark moods overtake me and the future looms with possible catastrophes, I look back over the years, my own and the world's, and I see how, when we've stumbled, God puts us on our feet once again. I echo the refrain from Cardinal Newman's hymn, "Lead, Kindly Light": "So long thy power hath blest me, sure it still will lead me on."

For I am convinced that neither death nor life, neither angels nor demons, neither the present nor the future, nor any powers, neither height nor depth, nor anything else in all creation will be able to separate us from the love of God in Christ Jesus our Lord.

Romans 8:38–39

5

When Rumors Distress You

How disturbed should you be by rumors? That depends on whether the rumor damages you or someone else. If someone else is being hurt, it is your clear duty to do something to stop the rumor's spread. If it's a threat to you alone, there may be better ways to deal with it than becoming distressed and striking back.

I've known people who go to the defense of others and hardly ever bother to defend themselves. They take almost literally the Lord's counsel, "If someone strikes you on the right cheek, turn to him the other also." They do this out of strength, not weakness.

But rumors and gossip are damaging. They grow like cancer. What began as a small lie soon becomes bloated into a big one. It is but common sense to nip it in the bud—without vindictiveness and with concern for all, even for whomever started it.

I remember as a boy being the victim of a rumor. A village storekeeper told someone I had stolen something from his shelves. The rumor reached my father. He asked me if it was true. When I said no, he marched me at once into the store and had the storekeeper apologize to me. I don't remember being especially upset by the rumor, but I do remember how gratifying it was to have my father trust me and come to my defense.

Whenever the gossip about you is untrue, you have the comfort of knowing that your integrity is not at stake. You are in the clear. Even so, the talk may be hurting someone dear to you. A husband, for instance, charged falsely with infidelity, may need to guard his wife and family from anguish by squelching the rumor.

It is a sad commentary on human nature that most of us tend to enjoy hearing something bad about people. We have a hard time resisting the urge to pass on the wretched tidbit to others. We say, "I don't know whether it's true, but have you heard. . . ?"

Nor is it uncommon even for the press to take a rumor and pass it on with introductions such as "It is alleged," "It is rumored," or "It is reported from an unconfirmed source." More than likely, what follows is not some eulogy to a person's goodness.

We must guard ourselves therefore from cynicism and disillusionment when we become victims of rumor. This is par for the course in a fallen world such as ours, inhabited by people such as we.

There are three courses to follow to reduce the damage of rumor.

First, be vigilant that you neither begin one nor repeat one. In commenting on the eighth commandment, "You shall not bear false witness against your neighbor," Luther gives this counsel: "That we do not tell lies about our neighbors, betray or slander them, or destroy their reputations. Instead we are to come to their defense, speak well of them, and interpret everything they do in the best possible light."

Second, come to the defense of anyone who is victimized by gossip.

Third, if you are the victim, remind yourself of two things. You have no guilt because you did no wrong. This in itself is profound comfort. Then remember that truth tends to create its own defense, and that the innocent one is often vindicated by history. Truth will out. You may not need to bother to defend truth or yourself.

Best of all, you can face God with a good conscience.

> *Do not let any unwholesome talk come out of your mouths,*
> *but only what is helpful for building others up according to*
> *their needs, that it may benefit those who listen.*
> *Ephesians 4:29*

6

When You Fear Growing Old

I'm frank to say that I fear growing too old. But when is too old? My uncle at ninety-six has diminished powers of seeing and hearing, but a sharp mind. Has he grown too old?

Fear is nothing new for me. I had anxieties and fears in high school. I certainly had them when I was responsible for my work and for my growing family. The fears of adolescence have now given way to the fears of aging. I rather think I prefer the ones I have now.

It startled me to read that of all people who have lived to be sixty-five since the dawn of history, more than 25% are still alive. And our crowd is growing. Having passed three score and ten, I now have less fear of dying than of living too long. I think of languishing in a nursing home, my memory largely gone and my usefulness to anyone in serious question.

My great-grandfather died at ninety-three and was sound of mind, my grandparents (whom I knew well) died swiftly in their eighties with no long prelude of illness, and my parents were only sixty-six when death struck them down. I have little family experience with lingering old age.

The four years since I officially left my desk and became classified as retired have been among the best years, if not the best. Both my wife and I are in good health. We've had the leisure to focus on each other and on our sprawling family of children and grandchildren, and on friends old and new. No longer do I have continuous, pervasive responsibility for a school or a parish.

I've been puzzled, and not a little impatient, with everybody insisting that we think about the sociobiologic issues of getting old on the one hand, and the problems of death and dying on the other. Why not just let us grow old, and when the time comes just let us die, without making it a duty to think about it too much?

This sounds naïve, I realize, and almost irresponsible. Caring for and making use of the increasing number of older people certainly are inescapable issues for government, church, and industry. And I am willing to cooperate in the wisdom that may emerge from the studies. But I find myself comfortable with the tempo of the years.

Autumn has always been my favorite season, even when I was young. The drama of life begins to wind down and the stage begins to empty. Birds wing south, the sun becomes a bit lazy, and the leaves don their riotous best for their silent requiem. Nature becomes serene and calm, and invites the human spirit to join her. The winter of sleep is near, but winter itself we know is but an interlude. The poet's question, "If winter comes, can spring be far behind?" is a promise.

No doubt I have been conditioned to old age by my grandfather, who in many ways was my companion from the time I can remember until I left for college. I never saw him work. I see him still, with a book and pipe, in the summer shade under the elm, or on the porch, or ambling up to the mailbox with his cane well before the mail arrived. I'm fascinated again by the memory of his accounts of the pioneer days and of his boyhood in Norway. I can never remember him saying a harsh or cynical word. For me he was the symbol of wisdom, strength, piety, compassion— even humor. If this was what growing old could mean, why shouldn't a boy long for that day?

I try not to fight against the ebbing strength, nor protest the aches and pains of worn parts that have done good work. I'm glad for the medical repairs to keep them going a bit longer. Why should I have the lusty appetite of thirty, or the ready sex, or the muscles tingling for a race with my grandchildren? "Grandpa, remember your age!" I'm told that brain cells do not give up so quickly, and I'm glad.

A friend of mine, a program director in a large hospital, told me, "Al, we've made an idolatry of life." He believes there's something basically wrong, and certainly counterproductive for happiness, with our almost pathological eagerness to outmaneuver death. I was struck with the truth of his observation one evening when a group of us older friends had been visiting. Suddenly I realized that for an hour we had been talking about nothing but diets, exercise, calories, cholesterol, pills, insomnia, and surgeons. We hadn't yet come to morticians. Evidently we were counting on escaping them.

Death is in the offing. There's nothing new about that. If we have allowed each day to bring its opportunities for service and joy (and a bit of pain), with minimum concern for the next day's menu, and if we have not lost sight of our Lord's promise that the next chapter of life will be immeasurably more wonderful than this one, we can enjoy being carried along on the stream of life, and take pleasure in the silent flow of time, making merry with the fellow passengers God gives us.

> *"Even to your old age and gray hairs I am he, I am he who will sustain you."*
> *Isaiah 46:4*

7

When You Wonder If Your Life Has Counted

With advancing years, people often look back and wonder if their lives have added up to anything significant. Is the world any better for their having lived? Couldn't the world have gotten along very well without them?

Alfred B. Nobel discovered dynamite a century ago. If today he could assess his amazing discovery, would he be able to balance off the good dynamite has done (in mining, for instance) against the bombs that have killed hundreds of thousands? Every advance in science presents us with this dilemma. Would even Orville and Wilbur Wright, who set the stage for air travel at Kitty Hawk in 1903, wonder if they might better have left us with the less hectic tempo of trains and ships?

Few of us have dramatically altered the shape of life by

what we have done. We've been able to accumulate money, for instance, or doubled the size of the farm. Has this done more good, or less, for us and for those who came after us?

Everybody can put some things in the credit column. You did do some good things, after all. But the moment you begin to count the good you might have done, but did-n't, and put this list in the debit column, you're uneasy. You'd like to forget all about striking any kind of balance.

But most of us cannot forget. Memories haunt us. Someone counted on us, and we didn't come through. We were too busy, or we were afraid to get involved. In Jesus' familiar parable of the Good Samaritan, one wonders how the priest and the Levite came to terms with the memory of having left the poor man in the ditch. Our lives may be lit-tered by such missed opportunities.

Quite apart from specific instance, every father will wonder if he was a good father. Every mother will wonder if she was a good mother. Even if the verdict of their chil-dren is an unconditional yes, they'll still wonder.

A friend of mine, an able surgeon, expressed his misgiv-ings about what he was doing. He said, "I'm but a high-grade plumber. I cut and stitch and patch, and give them a chance to live again. But I have nothing to do with why they should live. Why should they live?"

I had no easy answer. After all, is the goal of life simply to keep our hearts beating and our feet walking? Our almost pathetic preoccupation with health care may be a symptom of having no answer. Is it a triumph to fill our nursing homes with people who no longer recognize even their children?

Once we search for a bigger answer than simply to live, eat, and sleep well, to continue life to another generation, to work and play, we are on the trail of the meaning of life itself. Why should anything exist at all?

Nor will it be enough to say that we live in order to have more pleasure than pain, more happiness than sorrow. If that were the answer, the whole of existence could be a huge blunder. An impartial judge would say that throughout humanity's long history, the cargo of pain far outweighs the fleeting moments of pleasure. Even in our age, when we obviously have adequate food and shelter, how do we measure the loneliness, the fears, the frustrations, the shame, the regrets that burden great numbers of people?

40

The church founders had an answer: The measure of life is to glorify God and to serve him and to enjoy him forever. Whether you are rich or poor, learned or unlearned, powerful or dispossessed, whether you've known mostly sorrow or mostly joy, your life has great and ultimate meaning if it is nestled in God and in doing God's will.

Someone will protest, "That's a religious answer, and doesn't come to terms with the hard stuff of sickness and poverty and failure, or even with what happens to the world." Yes it does seem to shift the scene from survival of corporations and nations, from the size of your farm, from the promotions you've had, from the estate you may leave your children.

This answer reminds you that you are an eternal being, with a short tenure on this planet. You are a citizen of an imperishable kingdom. And your life will be measured by the standards of that kingdom. These standards call for love and honesty and mercy, whether they produce immediate prosperity and happiness or pain and sorrow. The goal is no longer security or survival. The goal is service. "The one who serves is greatest," said Jesus.

Instinctively, every person knows there's greater joy in giving service than in receiving service. "It is more blessed to give than to receive," said Jesus. My friend had discovered this. He said, "It's more fun to write a check than to get one. It's more fun to distribute than to accumulate." A great executive will look back with more joy on those instances when he has helped someone in need, encouraged someone whose courage was flagging, allayed the grief of someone who was weeping, than on the success of his corporation.

Of course, even if we shift our standards to those of the kingdom, our balances may still be in trouble. Did we give more comfort than pain? In this competitive world, did we crush more people than we encouraged? Were we compassionate or indifferent? Will we have left the world a better place for having lived? What will be the verdict of an all-knowing God?

It is at this point that the deep truths of our Christian faith come to our rescue. God alone can balance the debits and credits of our lives, and he does not even bother to see the ledger. We are God's sons and daughters, ledgers or no ledgers. God loves us, no matter what. God created us in love, God redeemed us in love, God claims us in love. This is the word that comes from that cross on Golgotha nearly 2000 years ago.

God hopes that we may not be lost in the jungle of bigger businesses and farms, bigger gross national products, bigger salaries, bigger wardrobes, bigger offices, bigger cars and boats. God knows (and so do we, really) that happiness and security do not lie there. Certainly the worth of a life does not lie there.

God weeps when we leave him and are lost in the jungle. God hopes that we will never lose sight of the kind world, the gentle encouragement, the warm sympathy, the helping hand, the healing forgiveness. These are the stuff of our humanity, the touch of the divine on earth, the key to the joys of heaven itself.

In the vast economy of God's empire, one kind deed, one effort for justice and mercy, can never be lost. These count for eternity.

> *Let us not become weary in doing good, for at the proper time*
> *we will reap a harvest if we do not give up.*
> *Galatians 6:9*

For Further Reading

The Color of the Night: Reflections on Suffering and the Book of Job
Gerhard E. Frost

The Art of Growing Old: A Guide to Faithful Aging
Carroll Saussy

Moving into a New Now: Faith for the Later Years
From the Journals of Mildred Tengbom

Jesus, Remember Me: Words of Assurance from Martin Luther
edited by Barbara Owen

Autumn Wisdom: Finding Meaning in Life's Later Years
James E. Miller

Liferails: Holding Fast to God's Promises
Scott Walker

All Will Be Well: A Gathering of Healing Prayers
edited by Lyn Klug

Our Hope for Years to Come: The Search for Spiritual Sanctuary
Reflections and Photographs
Martin Marty and Micah Marty